D1224313

Daring Explorers Who Sailed the Oceans

 Written by Roberta Stathis and Gregory Blanch

Ballard & Tighe

Brea, California

Daring Explorers Who Sailed the Oceans

SERIES EDITOR: HEERA KANG
PROJECT EDITOR: KRISTIN BELSHER
ART DIRECTOR: LILIANA ESTEP
GRAPHIC DESIGNER: RONALDO BENARAW
ILLUSTRATOR: GINA CAPALDI
EDITORIAL CONSULTANTS: PATRICE GOTSCH, JILL KINKADE
EDITORIAL STAFF: NINA CHUN, ALLISON MANGRUM
TECHNICAL PRINTING AND PRE-PRESS COORDINATOR: KATHLEEN STYFFE
PRINTING COORDINATOR: CATHY SANCHEZ

An IDEA® Book by Ballard & Tighe, Publishers
P.O. Box 219, Brea, CA 92822-0219

First Printing
ISBN 1-55501-548-4   Catalog #2-753

Contents

Introduction

Why do people leave their homes and risk their lives to explore the unknown? Christopher Columbus provided one explanation: "I went sailing upon the sea and have continued to this day ... to learn the secrets of the world." Of course, you have heard of Christopher Columbus, but what about Vasco da Gama? Amerigo Vespucci? Jacques Cartier? These men were all explorers who, like Columbus, sailed across the oceans hundreds of years ago.

From about 1450-1650—the period historians call the European age of exploration—the rulers of countries such as Portugal, Spain, and France were eager to find new routes to Asia. As their expeditions set sail for China and India, European explorers encountered continents they did not know existed, as well as highly developed civilizations in Africa, Asia, and the Americas.

Explorers included navigators, observers, and sailors, and this book is filled with stories of their curiosity, discovery, and determination. The men you will read about led the European age of exploration. They traveled or supported travel to unknown regions in search of new information and riches. Learn why these men wanted to explore the world and the consequences of their actions. Read interesting facts about their lives, and also find fun activities and experiments to try yourself.

As you read *Daring Explorers Who Sailed the Oceans* think about what you might explore some day.

PRINCE HENRY THE NAVIGATOR supported expeditions in the mid-1400s that explored the western coast of Africa. He is considered the leader of European exploration.

NORTH AMERICA

PACIFIC OCEAN

In 1497, VASCO DA GAMA sailed around the tip of Africa, finding an eastern route to India for the king of Portugal.

CHRISTOPHER COLUMBUS
landed in the New World in 1492.
He was exploring a western
sea route to Asia.

AMERIGO VESPUCCI
observed that North and South
America were continents. In 1499,
he sailed on a voyage that explored
South America.

EUROPE

ASIA

ATLANTIC
OCEAN

AFRICA

PACIFIC
OCEAN

SOUTH
AMERICA

INDIAN
OCEAN

N

W   E

S

FERDINAND MAGELLAN
was the first person to sail around the
world. He found a western passage
to Asia across the Pacific Ocean
in 1519.

JACQUES CARTIER
searched for the Northwest Passage.
He landed in northeastern Canada in
1534 and claimed the land for France.

Time Line

Having a common system to date events helps us compare events occurring at the same time in different parts of the world. Many experts in the Western world use the B.C./A.D. dating system. This system dates events from the birth of Jesus Christ, a central figure in the Christian religion. Events that took place before his birth are referred to as "before Christ" or B.C. dates. Traditionally, the term B.C. begins to be used around the time when human beings began to lead a more settled life, about 11,000 years ago. A.D. stands for the Latin words *anno Domini,* a phrase that means "in the year of the Lord." A.D. dates are given to events that occurred after Jesus's birth. A growing number of historians, archaeologists, and other academics also use the terms B.C.E. and C.E. to refer to these same periods of time. B.C.E. stands for "before Christian era" or "before common era." C.E. refers to "Christian era" or "common era." Some academic experts even use the term B.P., which stands for "before present." When we are not exactly sure of the date of an event, we use the Latin word *circa* which means "about." *Circa* is abbreviated c.

■ 1430s—Prince Henry's expeditions sail down the western coast of Africa

A.D. **1400**

1492—Columbus makes his first ■ voyage to the New World

TIPS on Reading a Time Line

Find the beginning and end dates.

Look at the far left and far right sides of the time line. These dates show you the range of time you are focusing on. What is the range of time for this book?

Check if the time line includes both B.C. and A.D. dates.

This books focuses on A.D. dates. When you read a time line with B.C. dates, remember that starting from the left, the B.C. dates become lower until the "0." After that, the A.D. dates go higher.

Think of other events that happened around the same time.

In the time line below, you can see that Vasco da Gama and Amerigo Vespucci were on expeditions around the same time. But they did not explore the same place. As you read about the two explorers, think about how their experiences were the same and different.

Jump in!

Copy the time line onto a sheet of paper, but make the end date on the far right side extend to the present day. Insert yourself into the time line to see how long ago the events you are reading about happened. You also can include other important dates you have learned about.

1498—Vasco da Gama and his crew land in India

1519—Ferdinand Magellan names the Pacific Ocean

A.D. **1650**

1499—Amerigo Vespucci sails on a voyage to South America

1534—Jacques Cartier leads his first expedition to find the Northwest Passage

Life on the
High Seas

Throughout history, explorers have been curious about the world. During Europe's age of exploration, unlike ever before, governments and private companies organized explorations. Some saw exploration as a way to bring Christianity to "non-believers." Others were interested in fame and adventure. However, the primary purpose of most explorations during this period was to find riches. This resulted in great wealth for European countries and made possible incredible cultural and scientific exchanges. However, there also were negative consequences. The actions of this period had far-reaching effects on the world.

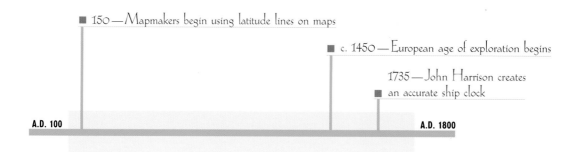

■ 150—Mapmakers begin using latitude lines on maps

■ c. 1450—European age of exploration begins

1735—John Harrison creates
■ an accurate ship clock

A.D. 100   A.D. 1800

During the European age of exploration, daring men sailed across the oceans in search of new routes to Asia. This early 20th century oil painting by American artist N.C. Wyeth shows his idea of one of Christopher Columbus's ships at sea.

A Sailor's World

Sailors on voyages of exploration lived hard and dangerous lives. Men could be at sea for months or even years! Many men died on voyages. But they were willing to **endure** hardships, dangers, and even death in order to achieve their goals—spreading Christianity, finding fame, and becoming rich.

On voyages, the captain was responsible for the ship. His officers—the pilot and first mate—gave him information about the position of the ship and supervised the sailors. Each day, the captain and officers would write detailed information about how far they had traveled, the direction they had taken, other ships they had seen, or **landmarks** they had passed. Ordinary sailors spent most of their time working. They took turns "on watch," looking for landmarks, changes in weather, and other ships. However, sailors did have some free time on these voyages of exploration. Often sailors spent their spare time gambling. A few read, but most sailors did not know how to read. Some played musical instruments to entertain themselves and the ship's crew.

There wasn't much room on the ship, but each sailor kept his few possessions in a sea chest. Sailors did not have beds. Sometimes, they used a hanging bed called a hammock, which looks like a big fish net with each end tied to a post. Fresh food, like cheese and fruit, rotted quickly. The ship carried barrels of salted meat and fish, and lots of ship biscuits, rice, and beans. The ship also carried barrels of water and wine. However, the barrels often leaked and supplies usually ran low. On long voyages where sailors could not get fresh fruits or vegetables, many got a disease called scurvy, caused by a diet lacking in vitamin C. There were no bathrooms onboard and not much fresh food or water, but there were plenty of rats and roaches.

endure: to carry on despite hardships; to put up with

landmark: a fixed marker; a large and identifying feature of a landscape

The leaders on the voyages were the captain and his officers. The captain was responsible for the ship. His officers gave him information about the ship's position and supervised the other sailors.

11

Navigating with Instruments

horizontal: relating to the horizon, the line where the earth and sky seem to meet

parallel: always the exact distance apart; parallel lines never cross one another

rely: to depend upon or trust; to use

Sailors during the European age of exploration did not have accurate maps of the world. They **relied** on simple navigational instruments, their knowledge of the sea, and their experience. From A.D. 150, mapmakers used **horizontal** grid lines to show different points on the earth's surface. These horizontal lines, sometimes called "parallels" because they are **parallel** to each other, are lines of latitude. They helped sailors determine their position north or south of the equator. Determining latitude was relatively easy. Using instruments such as the quadrant and cross staff, navigators could measure the distance of the sun and stars above the horizon. Sailors also relied on compasses to figure out their ship's course and direction. The Portuguese made improvements to the compass that made it more accurate.

Sailors used instruments such as the quadrant, shown in this modern illustration, to determine a ship's latitude.

Finding Longitude: Difficult!

Finding the east-west position, called longitude, was more difficult for sailors. To find their longitude, sailors needed to compare the time onboard the ship to the time at a specific location on land. Knowing the time onboard the ship was simple—as long as it was not a cloudy day! Sailors would simply reset their ship's clock every day at noon when the sun reached its highest point. However, sailors did not have a way to know the time at a specific location on land. They needed a clock that could be set on land and keep the correct time of that location throughout the voyage. Ship clocks at that time were inaccurate because of the weather and movement of the ship. It wasn't until the 1700s that the problem of determining longitude was solved. An Englishman named John Harrison invented a clock that kept accurate time onboard a ship. Harrison's clock, called a chronometer, was tested in 1761-1762.

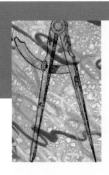

Look to the Source

Sailors depended on improved navigational instruments, but they also understood the importance of observation. Below is an excerpt from instructions that Spanish explorer Pedro de Queiros wrote for his voyage in 1606. He describes how to know if land is nearby.

"If the sea appears greasy, with leaves of trees, grass, herbs, wood, branches, palm nuts, and other things which the waves carry from the shores and rivers send down when in flood, it is a land being near ... If the sea is of any other color than the ordinary one of the ocean where there is great depth, namely, dark blue, it is necessary to exercise care, and much more if at night the sea should be heard to make sounds greater than is usual."

Far-Reaching Consequences

European explorers traveled to many new places and made great advances in their knowledge of geography and navigation. Their explorations brought great wealth to European countries and brought together different parts of the world. These **expeditions** made possible the exchange of plants, animals, technology, culture, and ideas. These exchanges had major economic and social effects on Europe, Africa, Asia, and the Americas.

Of course, these effects were not all positive, especially for the people of Africa and the Americas. Much of their land was taken over by European countries. Millions died from diseases, many were forced to become slaves, and many cultures and traditions were destroyed. However, the explorers of this age probably did not foresee or intend these consequences of their exploration. Theirs are stories of courageous men curious about the world, able to endure hardships, and willing to risk their lives to explore the unknown.

expedition: a trip made by a group of people for a specific purpose

Quick Quiz

1. What was the typical job of a sailor?

2. What kinds of instruments were needed to measure latitude?

3. A sailor's life was difficult and uncomfortable. Why do you think so many men were eager to become sailors?

4. Reread the Look to the Source excerpt and put it into your own words. Do you think sailors today still depend on observation? Why or why not?

Just for Fun!

Make Ship Biscuits

Ship biscuits were one of the most important foods in a sailor's diet during the European age of exploration. Sailors did not hand down a written recipe for ship biscuits. However, the recipe below is probably very close to the one they used.

Ingredients:
- 2 cups flour (semolina flour works best)
- ½ cup water
- salt to taste

Directions:

Step 1: Mix the flour and salt together; stir in the water.

Step 2: Place the dough on a lightly floured board and knead for about three minutes.

Step 3: Roll out the dough until it is ½-inch thick. Then cut the dough into two-inch pieces, using a knife or cookie cutter.

Step 4: Place the biscuits on a baking sheet and poke holes in them with a fork or the tip of a knife.

Step 5: Bake at 250 degrees for one hour or until lightly browned. Let biscuits cool. Store them in an airtight container. Makes about 12-15 biscuits.

Prince Henry
the Navigator

Prince Henry of Portugal could have lived a life of luxury. Instead, curious about the unknown, he spent his life helping others explore new lands. Although he is called Henry "the Navigator," he never led a ship and only sailed on three voyages. He is considered to be the leader of early European exploration. Prince Henry set the stage for the great European explorations that followed.

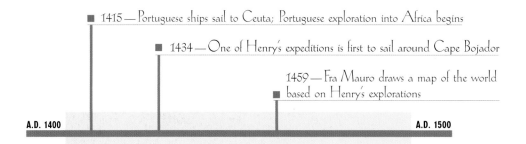

1415 — Portuguese ships sail to Ceuta; Portuguese exploration into Africa begins

1434 — One of Henry's expeditions is first to sail around Cape Bojador

1459 — Fra Mauro draws a map of the world based on Henry's explorations

A.D. 1400   A.D. 1500

Henry the Navigator was eager to help others explore new lands. This illustration is a modern artist's idea of how Prince Henry—shown measuring distance on a map—might have looked.

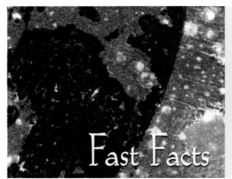
NAME: Prince Henry of Portugal; also called Henry the Navigator
BORN: 1394; Oporto, Portugal
DIED: 1460; Sagres, Portugal
SAILED FOR: Portugal
EXPLORED: The western coast of Africa by supporting explorations

Iberian Peninsula: the region of southwestern Europe that is surrounded on three sides by water; present-day Spain and Portugal

knight: during the Middle Ages in Europe, a soldier on horseback, usually of noble birth, who fought for a ruler and who was given land and privileges in return

Young Prince Henry

Henry's parents, King John I and Queen Philippa, were the rulers of Portugal, a small kingdom on the **Iberian Peninsula**. King John had been fighting hard to bring together the people in his kingdom. He also had been fighting against invading armies from other kingdoms. Finally, in 1385, King John united the people of Portugal.

The king and queen had six children—five boys and one girl. Henry was the third son. He was born in March of 1394 in Oporto, Portugal. Henry and his brothers were well educated. In addition to Portuguese, they learned Greek, Latin, and French. When Henry was about 17, Portugal was a prosperous country. There were no wars, everyone in the royal family was healthy, and the three older boys, including Henry, had become **knights**.

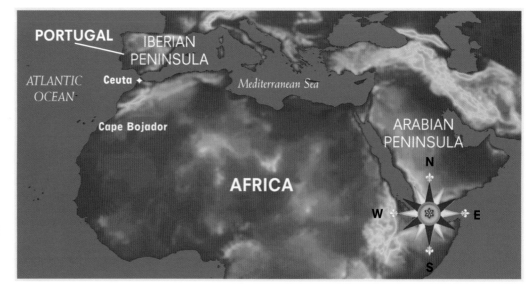

One of Prince Henry's most famous expeditions sailed around Cape Bojador and traveled far down the African coast. No other European exploration had gone that far south before.

Henry's First Adventure

The king wanted to celebrate his good fortune. He decided to hold a sporting event called a jousting tournament. In a jousting tournament, two knights on horseback, each carrying a **lance**, try to knock one another to the ground. The king's sons, however, were not interested in a sporting event. They wanted a real fight. They convinced their father that Portugal should capture the North African city of Ceuta (SAY-oo-tah). **Arab** traders ruled the city. If Henry and his brothers were successful, they would gain control of Ceuta's trade. For three years they prepared to fight. Then, in 1415, the Portuguese **fleet** sailed to Ceuta and captured the city. However, Portugal did not gain control of the trade. The Arab traders simply moved their business to another city. It was a partial victory, and the beginning of Portuguese expansion in Africa.

Arab: a person of the Arabian Peninsula

fleet: a group of ships

lance: a weapon with a long wooden pole and a sharp metal point

The Portuguese captured the Arab trade city of Ceuta in 1415. This modern illustration is based on a picture in a book about cities made in 1572.

19

Henry's School of Navigation

After the capture of Ceuta, Henry returned to Portugal. He decided that if he could not force the Arabs to trade, he would try to **bypass** them completely. To do this, he had to sail along the African coastline farther south than any European had gone before. To learn how to make this kind of trip, he invited sailors and shipbuilders to come to Portugal where he started a school of navigation. At this school, sailors, shipbuilders, mapmakers, astronomers, and others could share their knowledge of sea travel. Henry assembled every known map he could find. He encouraged the men at the school to develop new sailing tools that helped sailors determine their exact position at sea.

When Henry thought his students were ready to explore the unknown coastline, he sent them off on expeditions. Sailors were told to write down what they saw and to make drawings of the land and other geographical features. Henry was interested in knowing about the tides, **reefs**, landmarks, harbors, the color of the water, and other information that would help future expeditions. Never before had sailors recorded this kind of information in a systematic way.

bypass: to go around instead of going through; to avoid an obstacle

reef: a ridge of rocks, sand, or coral that rise to or near the surface of a body of water

20

Builders at Prince Henry's school invented a new type of ship called a caravel. Early caravels were more like Arab ships than European ships of the time. These ships were faster and easier to control than European ships.

Exploring the African Coast

Legend said the water boiled red with blood beyond Cape Bojador, in northwestern Africa. By 1434 one of Henry's expeditions decided to take the risk, and for the first time ever Europeans sailed around the cape. This was an important **milestone**. They did not find red boiling blood! With each trip, Henry's sailors sailed farther south down the African coast. On one trip, the sailors left their ship and went inland on horseback. They were attacked by people living in the area. When the sailors returned to Portugal to report this to Henry, he told them to go back and make friends with the Africans they had encountered. Instead, the sailors captured about 10 Africans and brought them back to Portugal. Henry listened to the Africans tell about their land. He began to realize that Africa was a very large continent and that there was more land even farther south of where the sailors had explored. He released the prisoners and sent them home.

Look to the Source

Much of what we know about Prince Henry comes from the writings of Gomes Eanes de Zurara, the official reporter of Prince Henry's experiences. Below you can read an excerpt from the *Chronicle of Guinea*, which describes what happened to African slaves when they arrived at a Portuguese port in August 1444.

custom: the traditional way people do things

grief: great sadness

lament: to express sadness

piteously: sadly

"These people, assembled together on that open place, were an astonishing sight. ... Some held their heads low, their faces bathed in tears as they looked at each other; some groaned very **piteously** ... others struck their faces with their hands and threw themselves full length on the ground; yet others **lamented** in the form of a chant, according to the **custom** of their native land, and though the words of the language in which they sang could not be understood by our people, the chant revealed clearly enough the degree of their **grief** ..."

The African Slave Trade Begins

In other voyages, Henry's explorers discovered **uninhabited** islands off the western coast of Africa. They also set up trading posts along the coast. They traded wheat, cloth, iron knives, and other manufactured goods for African gold. Henry had accomplished his goal to bypass the Arabs and trade directly with Africans for gold.

This also was the beginning of the African slave trade. When an African ruler had no more gold to trade, he offered prisoners as slaves. In 1441, Portuguese explorers brought their first cargo of African slaves to Portugal. Soon, slaves were in high demand in Europe.

uninhabited: not having any people living there

After Portuguese explorers brought their first African slaves to Portugal, slaves were in demand in Europe. This woodcut illustration shows Africans captured by a Portuguese slave hunter.

colony: a group of
people who settle in a
land far away

Fra: brother; a title
given to an Italian
friar or monk;
abbreviation of the
Italian word *frate*

physical geography:
the study of the
earth's structures and
processes, including
land forms, climate,
and wind and ocean
currents

Setting the Stage for Exploration

By 1458, Henry's sailors had established many **colonies** along the western coast of Africa. At his school in Portugal, mapmakers were using the information from the voyages to draw new maps and charts. Astronomers and instrument makers were finding ways to improve navigational tools. In 1459, **Fra** Mauro—one of the greatest mapmakers Venice, Italy—completed a large map of the world based on the information Henry's explorers had gathered. This map showed the **physical geography** of the earth drawn with precise mathematics.

Henry died in 1460 when he was 66 years old. Portugal became a very rich country because of the explorations he supported. As you have read, in many ways, Henry is the man who began Europe's age of exploration. His efforts had far-reaching consequences. As a result of his explorations, the African slave trade began. But Henry's work also set the stage for the great voyages of explorers such as Christopher Columbus.

Quick Quiz

1. What city did Henry and his brothers convince the king to capture?

2. What were some of the consequences of Henry's exploration? How were they far-reaching?

3. Henry could have done anything with his life. Why do you think he started a school of navigation and encouraged exploration?

4. Reread the Look to the Source excerpt and put it in your own words. Do you think Zurara was simply providing a factual account of what he saw, or do you think he was touched by the suffering of the slaves?

Just for Fun!

Make a Compass

Sailors relied on compasses to figure out their ship's course. During the 1400s, improvements to navigational instruments helped sailors go farther on ocean voyages. For example, when sailors learned how to use the magnetic compass, they were better able to decide in which direction to steer their ships and stay on course. A magnetic compass has an iron needle that always points north. You can make your own magnetic compass following the directions below.

Materials Needed:
- a magnet
- a piece of cork
- a long, metal needle
- a small bowl of water

Directions:
First, rub the needle with the magnet 20-30 times in one direction (see picture 1). Test if the needle is magnetized by using it to pick up a staple or small paper clip. Next, carefully push the needle through the middle of the piece of cork (see picture 2). Then, float the cork in the bowl (see picture 3). The needle will point toward magnetic north!

1

2

3

Christopher Columbus

 hough a Portuguese prince started Europe's age of exploration, it is Christopher Columbus who receives the most attention. Columbus's voyage in 1492 remains one of the most famous voyages in history—at least in the English-speaking world. Why? Christopher Columbus was the first European to sail west across the Atlantic Ocean with the goal of reaching Asia. Today, not everyone considers him a hero, but almost all agree that Christopher Columbus played an important role in world history.

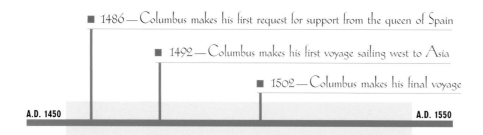

- 1486—Columbus makes his first request for support from the queen of Spain
- 1492—Columbus makes his first voyage sailing west to Asia
- 1502—Columbus makes his final voyage

A.D. 1450   A.D. 1550

26

Christopher Columbus arrived on the island of
San Salvador on October 12, 1492. This
picture, titled "Columbus Taking Possession of
the New Country," was created around 1893.

From Italy to Portugal

Christopher Columbus was born into a poor Italian family in 1451. His parents, Domenico and Susanna, named him Cristoforo Colombo. They raised him and his four **siblings** in the busy **port** city of Genoa. Growing up, Columbus probably visited the docks often to see the ships. Sometime before he turned 20, Columbus became a sailor on cargo ships that sailed the Mediterranean Sea. After five years on the calm waters of the Mediterranean, Columbus was ready to sail the Atlantic Ocean. He joined a crew headed for northern Europe. Everything went well until the ship sank as it was passing by Portugal's coast. Columbus had to swim six miles to the shore!

Back in Portugal, Columbus taught himself to read and write the language used by educated people in Portugal. He got married and started a family. During this time, he also began to think about finding a sea route to Asia by sailing west across the Atlantic Ocean. By that time, every educated person knew the world was round. And judging from the maps that existed at the time, it made sense to Columbus that he could reach Asia by sailing west.

port: a place by the sea or ocean where boats load and unload

sibling: brother or sister

Columbus was determined to find a western route to Asia across the Atlantic. Here you can see the route he took in 1492. The area where Columbus landed is enlarged.

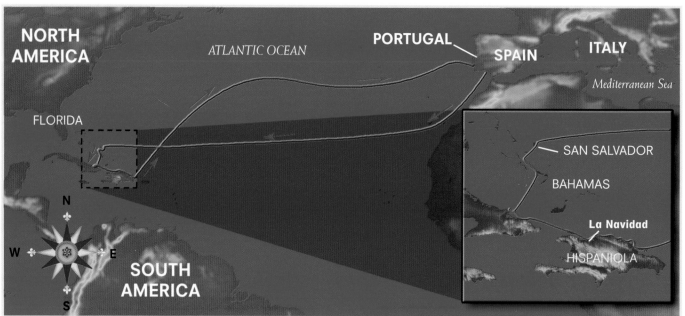

NORTH AMERICA

ATLANTIC OCEAN

PORTUGAL

SPAIN

ITALY

Mediterranean Sea

FLORIDA

SAN SALVADOR

BAHAMAS

La Navidad

HISPANIOLA

SOUTH AMERICA

N
W   E
S

NAME: Christopher Columbus
BORN: 1451 in Genoa, Italy
DIED: May 20, 1506 in Spain
SAILED FOR: Spain
EXPLORED: Western route to Asia; West Indies (present-day Caribbean islands)

Fast Facts

After a previous request, in 1492 the king and queen of Spain agreed to support Columbus's expedition. This image shows Columbus kneeling before Queen Isabella.

Searching for Support

Columbus needed support for this expensive and daring voyage west. At this time, kings and queens were about the only people who had money to invest in such risky projects. Columbus went first to the king of Portugal. However, the king's counselors advised against supporting Columbus. In 1485, after his wife's death, Columbus sailed to Spain with his young son Diego to meet with Queen Isabella and King Ferdinand. However, the king and queen were busy fighting a war. Columbus had to wait a year to present his plan to the queen. She listened to him and chose a group of advisors to study his plan, but nothing seemed to happen. Columbus decided to go back and ask the king of Portugal again for support. However, just as Columbus arrived in Portugal the explorer Bartolomeu Dias returned from his successful voyage around the southern tip of Africa. The Portuguese now had their sea route to Asia and had no need to find another route. Columbus still wanted to find a western sea passage to Asia. He decided to go back to Spain. In 1492, the king and queen of Spain agreed to support his expedition.

Setting Sail

On August 3, 1492, with three ships and 88 men, Christopher Columbus set sail west for Asia. Columbus commanded the largest ship, the *Santa María*. The other ships, the *Niña* and the *Pinta*, were smaller but faster caravels. Columbus kept a detailed journal of the voyage. It was a long and difficult trip across the Atlantic. Some of his crew became very frightened and wanted to return home. Columbus promised a coat as a reward to the first man to see land. He was certain they were close to their goal. Sure enough, on October 12, 1492, a sailor called out, *"Tierra!"*—the Spanish word for land.

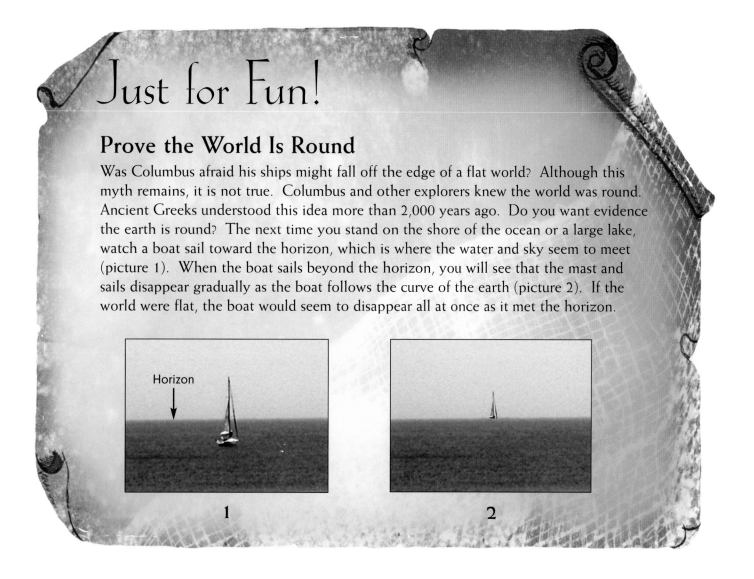

Just for Fun!

Prove the World Is Round

Was Columbus afraid his ships might fall off the edge of a flat world? Although this myth remains, it is not true. Columbus and other explorers knew the world was round. Ancient Greeks understood this idea more than 2,000 years ago. Do you want evidence the earth is round? The next time you stand on the shore of the ocean or a large lake, watch a boat sail toward the horizon, which is where the water and sky seem to meet (picture 1). When the boat sails beyond the horizon, you will see that the mast and sails disappear gradually as the boat follows the curve of the earth (picture 2). If the world were flat, the boat would seem to disappear all at once as it met the horizon.

Horizon

1

2

The Famous Landing

New World: the
Western Hemisphere;
North and South
America and adjacent
islands

trinket: a small
inexpensive ornament,
such as a small piece
of jewelry

The three ships landed on an island in the Bahamas, just off the southern coast of present-day Florida. Columbus called the island San Salvador and claimed it for Spain. Columbus believed he had landed in Asia in a place called the Indies, and he called the friendly people who greeted him "Indians." These Indians, who were actually called the Arawaks, brought parrots, cotton thread, and other gifts to Columbus. In return, he gave the people red caps and beads and other **trinkets**. The expedition then sailed on to other islands. They had to stop when the *Santa María* wrecked off the shore of an island called Hispaniola. The Arawaks who lived on the island helped the Europeans gather wood from the wreckage. Columbus's crew, with help from the Arawaks, then built a fort called La Navidad on the island. Some of Columbus's crew stayed at La Navidad. The others returned to Spain with Columbus.

From Honor to Shame

Once in Spain, Columbus immediately sent a letter to the king and queen telling them of his voyage. They invited him to their court, and treated him like a hero. The king and queen eagerly supported Columbus's second voyage to the **New World**. Columbus left Spain in the fall of 1493. When he arrived in Hispaniola, he found that the fort La Navidad was destroyed and the crew was gone! Columbus learned that his men had mistreated the Arawaks. The Arawaks fought back and killed the crew. Columbus rebuilt the settlement, but it soon began to have problems as well.

This time, when Columbus returned to Spain, he did not receive a hero's welcome. Other explorers had made discoveries, and Columbus's voyage did not seem as great as it once had. However, he went on a third voyage in 1498 and explored more islands. Then, news reached Isabella and Ferdinand that the settlement on Hispaniola was in trouble. The official they sent to look into the matter arrested Columbus and brought him back to Spain in chains. The king and queen released Columbus, but they were no longer very interested in him.

Look to the Source

Below you can read an excerpt from Columbus's journal. This entry was written on October 13, 1492. It tells of Columbus's first encounter with the native people of Hispaniola—the Arawaks.

"As soon as it dawned, many of these people came to the beach—all young as I have said. … They brought balls of spun cotton and parrots and **javelins** and other little things that it would be tiresome to write down. … This island is quite big and very flat with very green trees and much water and a very large lake in the middle and without any mountains; and all of it so green that it is a pleasure to look at. And these people are very gentle, and because of their desire to have some of our things, … everything they have they give for anything given to them, for they traded even for pieces of bowls and broken glass cups. …"

javelin:
a spear

On his expeditions, Columbus encountered native people called the Arawaks.

"History knows of no man who ever did the like, wherefore the world will ever remember the first discoverer of the West Indies."
—Columbus's son, Ferdinand, c. 1539

A Final Voyage, a Lasting Legacy

Despite the problems, Isabella and Ferdinand agreed to support Columbus on one last voyage. In 1502, Columbus and his crew headed back across the Atlantic Ocean. However, the ships he had were old and not very seaworthy. The expedition was forced to stay on an island for almost a year before they were rescued. Columbus returned to Spain, an old and sick man. Soon after, Queen Isabella died. Columbus wanted the attention and riches he thought he deserved, but King Ferdinand would have nothing to do with him. Columbus died on May 20, 1506, with only his family and closest friends at his bedside.

Columbus's voyages across the Atlantic had many consequences for Europe and the Americas. However, the name of the continent that Columbus "discovered" belongs to another Italian explorer.

Quick Quiz

1. When Columbus returned to Hispaniola on his second voyage, what had happened to his crew?

2. Why do people disagree about whether Christopher Columbus was a hero? Why do they agree that he played an important role in world history?

3. Reread the Look to the Source excerpt and describe it in your own words. Why do you think the Arawaks wanted the things Columbus and his men had? Why do you think Columbus and his men wanted the things the Arawaks had?

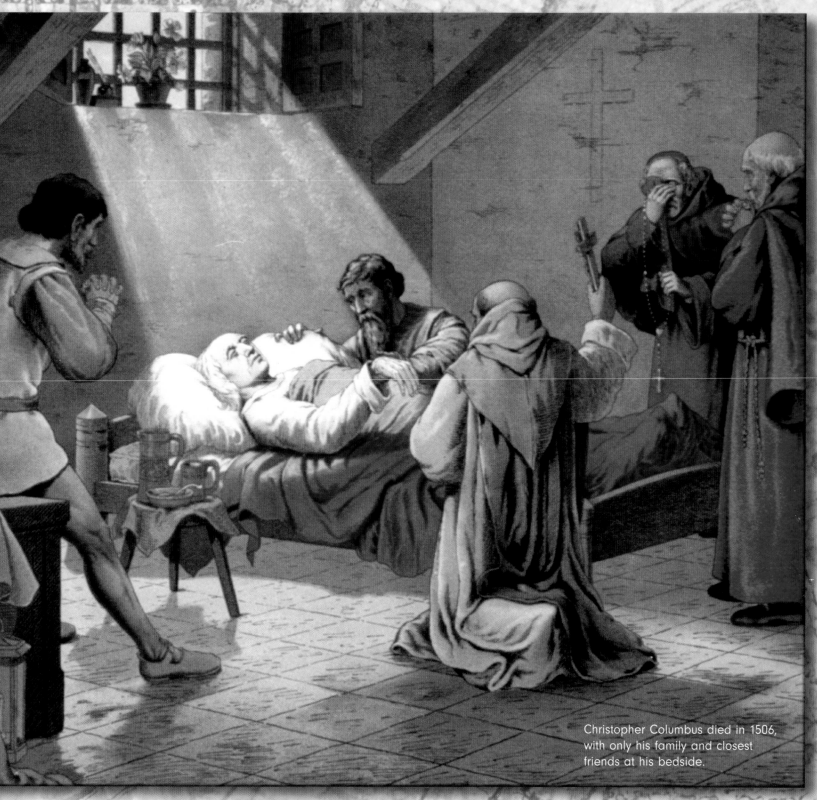

Christopher Columbus died in 1506, with only his family and closest friends at his bedside.

Amerigo Vespucci

Christopher Columbus gets most of the credit for being the first European to "discover" America. Some people think it was unfair that the continents people learned about because of Columbus were named after someone else. We don't live on the continent of North Columbus. We live in North America. America? Where did that name come from? The answer is Amerigo Vespucci, an Italian explorer born in Florence around 1454.

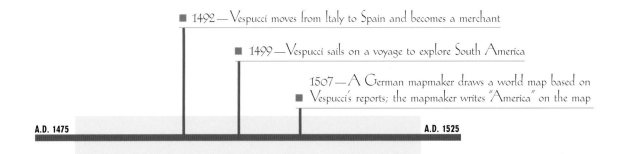

■ 1492 — Vespucci moves from Italy to Spain and becomes a merchant

■ 1499 — Vespucci sails on a voyage to explore South America

1507 — A German mapmaker draws a world map based on
■ Vespucci's reports; the mapmaker writes "America" on the map

A.D. 1475   A.D. 1525

Amerigo Vespucci was the first explorer to report that North and South America were new lands and not part of Asia.

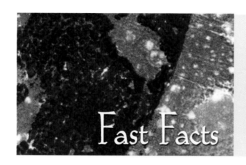
NAME: Amerigo Vespucci
BORN: c. 1454 in Florence, Italy
DIED: 1512 in Seville, Spain
SAILED: On Spanish and Portuguese ships
EXPLORED: North and South America

Excited about Exploring the World

Historians do not know much about the early life of Amerigo Vespucci (ves-POO-chee). They do know that in 1492, he moved to Seville, Spain and became a merchant. It appears that he had both successes and failures in this line of work. Vespucci once said of the life of a merchant, "**perishable** property, unevenly distributed, can one day carry man up to heights, only to let him down on the next." Eventually, he was probably influenced by the excitement of exploration that seemed to affect everyone in Spain during this time. Spain was a center of activity for European explorers. There, Vespucci met and became friends with many sailors and explorers, including Christopher Columbus. Vespucci made his own voyage to the New World in 1499.

perishable: something that spoils or rots easily

"I resolved to abandon trade and to fix my aim on something more praiseworthy ... going to see part of the world and its wonders ... to aid in making discovery."
—Amerigo Vespucci, 1497

A Writer, Not a Sailor

Amerigo Vespucci was not a sailor. He led no expeditions. Instead, he was onboard ships as a **representative** of his **Florentine** employer. Lorenzo di Pierfrancesco di Medici supported Vespucci on expeditions and expected him to report on the achievements and problems of the voyages. The purpose of these expeditions was to search for a new route to Asia. While most sailors onboard the ships could barely sign their own names, Vespucci was an educated man and a good writer. His writing was detailed and vivid. He described how the ship he was on "sailed for two months and two days across the vast ocean under a sky so dark and stormy that neither sun nor moon was visible."

Florentine: someone who lives in Florence, Italy

representative: a person acting on behalf of the interests of another person

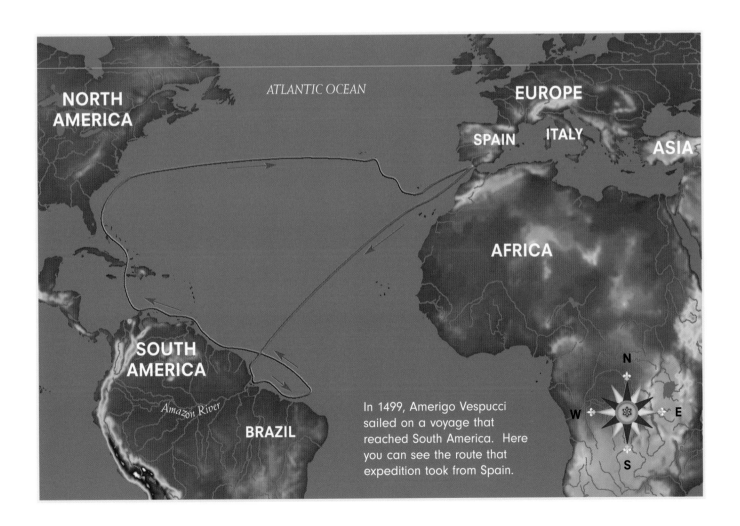

In 1499, Amerigo Vespucci sailed on a voyage that reached South America. Here you can see the route that expedition took from Spain.

Exploring the *Mundus Novus*

ancestor: a family member who lived a long time ago

mouth: the place where a river meets a sea or ocean

patron: a person who supports, protects, or champions something

On his first voyage, Vespucci explored the **mouth** of the Amazon River in South America. It was on this trip that Vespucci discovered that this land was too far south to be Asia. He began to realize the landmasses we call South America and North America were not part of Asia, as Columbus believed. They were separate continents. Vespucci wrote a letter to his **patron** about this discovery. He titled his letter *Mundus Novus*, which means "New World." Vespucci wrote, "For none of our **ancestors** had any knowledge of the countries we saw ... Most of them believed that no mainland existed south of the equator; that there were only endless stretches of sea ..." Vespucci's letter was intended only for Lorenzo di Pierfrancesco di Medici, but it was quickly translated and read by others. Reports of Vespucci's voyages soon spread across Europe. A much wider audience was interested in knowing the details of the expedition. Vespucci's writing gave readers the sense that they were on the adventure with him, and his reports contained valuable information about the geography of the new lands. His letter also gave some people the idea that Vespucci, not Columbus, was the first person to explore the Americas.

Look to the Source

Below is an excerpt from a letter that Amerigo Vespucci wrote to his patron Lorenzo di Pierfrancesco di Medici in March or April 1503.

clemency: mercy

trending: turning in one direction

"We knew that land to be a continent, and not an island, from its long beach extending without **trending** round, the numerous tribes and people, the numerous kinds of wild animals unknown in our country, and many others never seen before by us. ... The **clemency** of God was shown forth to us by being brought to these regions; for the ships were in a leaking state, and in a few days our lives might have been lost in the sea. ..."

Amerigo Vespucci was not a sailor; he was an observer and a writer. This modern illustration shows Vespucci holding a navigational instrument that would have been used by sailors during this time.

New World is Named America

namesake: a person or thing named after another

Meanwhile, a nobleman in a little town in France gathered together a number of scholars. Among the scholars was a young German mapmaker named Martin Waldseemüller. He produced a world map in 1507 showing the two continents that Amerigo Vespucci described in his letter. Waldseemüller wrote the name "America" in the margin of his map and across the area of present-day Brazil. Spain did not like the idea of naming the land *America*, but clearly it caught on. Amerigo Vespucci died in Seville in 1512 never knowing that he was the **namesake** for the continents North America and South America.

Quick Quiz

1. Who was the famous explorer that Amerigo Vespucci met in Spain?

2. What was Vespucci's role on the voyages he took to the New World?

3. What evidence does Vespucci use to support his argument that the land he was exploring was a new continent?

4. Reread the Look to the Source excerpt and tell what it means in your own words. Do you think Vespucci's account is entirely factual? Give examples to explain your answer.

42

Just for Fun!

Make a Family Map

Sailors during the European age of exploration used maps to find their way around the world. Explorers like Amerigo Vespucci even helped create more accurate maps by making new discoveries and reporting on what they found. Use the ideas below to make a map showing your family's own travels and explorations around the world.

Materials:
world map (go to www.ballard-tighe.com/readingbookactivities to download a map) • note pad • stickers • colored pens or pencils • colored yarn • photographs or drawings of family members • glue

Directions:
Arrange a time to talk with members of your family. You will need a world map and a notepad. Ask each person to show on the world map where they were born, places they have traveled, and other places they have lived. Ask older relatives where their parents and grandparents came from. Did they move from one country to another? Did they live on another continent? Take notes on each person's response.

When you have gathered all the information you need, decide how to display it on your map. For example, you might place a sticker or draw a house on the map to show where your family lives today (picture 1). Use colored markers or yarn to show places where your family has lived and traveled (picture 2). Place photographs or drawings of your family members on the map (picture 3). Give your map a title and display it for your family!

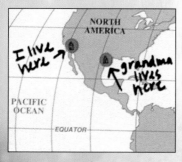

1

2

3

Vasco da Gama

bout the same time Christopher Columbus and Amerigo Vespucci explored the New World for Spain, another man was convincing Portugal to find an eastern sea route to India. Vasco da Gama shared the dream of many other young Portuguese sailors to find a sea route to Asia. He got his chance to pursue this dream when the king of Portugal chose him to lead an expedition to India.

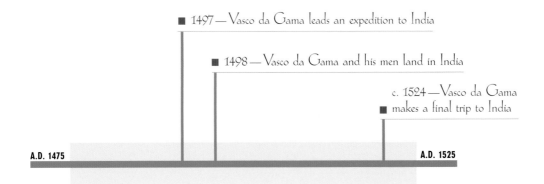

■ 1497—Vasco da Gama leads an expedition to India

■ 1498—Vasco da Gama and his men land in India

c. 1524—Vasco da Gama
■ makes a final trip to India

A.D. 1475   A.D. 1525

Vasco da Gama's expedition arrived in India in May 1498. This watercolor painting was created around 1880 by Ernesto Casanova. You can see da Gama holding a flag and pointing at land.

NAME: Vasco da Gama
BORN: c. 1468 in Sines, Portugal
DIED: December 24, 1524 in India
SAILED FOR: Portugal
EXPLORED: Eastern sea route to India

Prepared for Life at Sea

Vasco da Gama was born in the small Portuguese coast town of Sines around 1468. Unlike Columbus, da Gama's family was wealthy, and his father held an important position in the court of the Portuguese king. Da Gama grew up in a place where the sea was an important part of every aspect of life. He fished, swam, and sailed from an early age. Later, he became a soldier and also studied navigation.

Setting Sail for Asia

In 1496, the king of Portugal chose da Gama to lead an expedition to India. The king provided da Gama with four ships that together carried cannons, supplies, and goods to trade. In addition to da Gama, his officers, and sailors, the expedition included interpreters, priests, a historian, and carpenters.

On July 8, 1497, da Gama's expedition set sail for Asia. Church leaders were there to bless the voyage. Wives and children waved good-bye, not knowing if they would see their loved ones again. The ships sailed south to the Madeira Islands, then west toward South America. At the equator, the ships turned south again and then east in preparation to round the Cape of Good Hope at the southern end of Africa. Later, people learned this was the best sea route around the Cape of Good Hope. Historians believe da Gama, during this voyage, was the first European sea captain to use the southeast trade winds to cross the south Atlantic Ocean.

Landing in Africa

Before they rounded the Cape of Good Hope, one of the sailors sighted land! On November 4, 1497, the ships landed on the coast of southern Africa. They met a group of people, called Hottentots, who lived in the region. When fighting broke out between the two groups, da Gama and his men quickly set sail. They rounded the Cape of Good Hope and landed at Mossel Bay, where another group of Hottentots brought items to trade. However, after a friendly beginning, da Gama and his men left on bad terms with the Hottentots.

Da Gama and his crew sailed for 10 months before reaching India. This map shows the route the expedition took around the Cape of Good Hope to Asia.

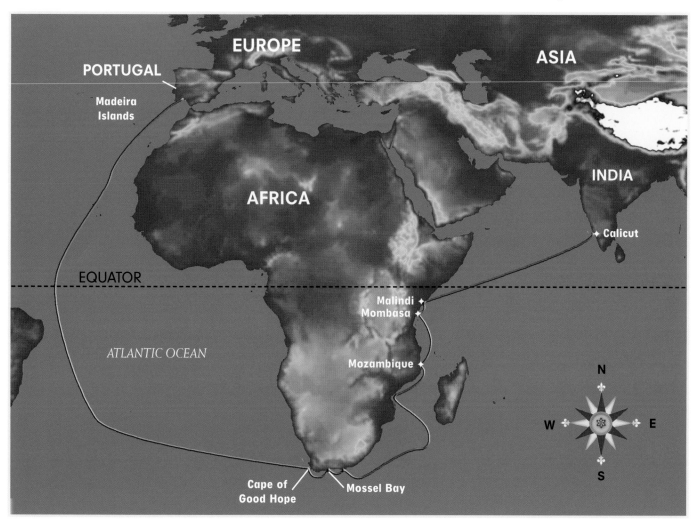

Along the African Coast

In order for the other three ships to be well supplied, da Gama decided to leave one of the ships behind. The expedition now sailed north along the eastern coast of Africa. No Portuguese explorer had ever sailed this far before. They landed again and were met by friendly Bantu people. By this time, many of da Gama's sailors were sick from scurvy. The Bantu gave them fruit, which helped them get well and continue on their journey. In early March 1498, the expedition arrived in the **Muslim** coastal city of Mozambique. Unfortunately for da Gama, the trading goods he brought—including olive oil, hats, bells, and bracelets—did not impress the merchants or the **sultan**. In fact, the merchants and the ruler were insulted by the trinkets and refused to trade. Da Gama's expedition arrived next in Mombasa. They were not welcomed there either.

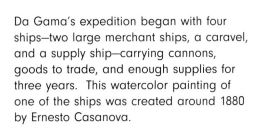

Da Gama's expedition began with four ships—two large merchant ships, a caravel, and a supply ship—carrying cannons, goods to trade, and enough supplies for three years. This watercolor painting of one of the ships was created around 1880 by Ernesto Casanova.

48

Look to the Source

Some of what we know about Vasco da Gama's voyage comes from a man named Gaspar Correa. Correa took part in da Gama's expedition and wrote a journal about his experiences. Historians think the journal contains many errors, but it still provides valuable information about the people, time, and place. You can read below a translated passage that describes one of the storms the sailors faced on da Gama's expedition.

fast: tied or held to something securely

lurch: to roll or sway suddenly, as a ship during a storm

rage: to happen with great intensity

"The seas rose towards the sky and fell back in heavy showers which flooded the ships. The storm **raging** thus violently, the danger was doubled, for suddenly the wind died out, so that the ships lay dead between the waves, **lurching** so heavily that they took in water on both sides; and the men made themselves **fast** not to fall from one side to the other; and everything in the ships was breaking up, so that all cried to God for mercy."

India at Last!

Finally, da Gama and his men were welcomed at the Muslim port city of Malindi. The sultan of Malindi gave the Portuguese food and spices in exchange for the trinkets. The sultan also gave da Gama a skilled seaman who could show the Portuguese the way to India. Da Gama landed in Calicut, India on May 20, 1498. However, da Gama quickly realized that Arabs were already important trading partners with India. The ruler of Calicut agreed to sell da Gama food, but he did not want to insult his Arab trading partners by trading with the Portuguese. Moreover, the trinkets the Portuguese offered in trade did not impress him. Da Gama decided that the Portuguese would have to use force to get India to trade with Portugal. The expedition then set sail to return home.

The Long Trip Home

The expedition started the voyage home on August 29, 1498. The three-month trip back to Africa was terrible. Food and water ran out and many men died. Da Gama decided there were not enough men for his three ships. He burned one of the ships and divided the crew among the remaining two ships. The men sailed into Portugal at the end of August 1499. They had traveled more than 27,000 miles and were greeted by cheering crowds. The spices the expedition brought were worth a fortune, but only about one-fourth of the men who started the trip made it home.

Earning Many Honors

Da Gama went on another voyage and earned many honors before he retired in the early 1500s. Around 1524, the king of Portugal asked him to come out of retirement to help settle problems in India. Vasco da Gama died on December 24, 1524 just after he landed in India.

Vasco da Gama's first voyage was a milestone in world history. Soon after that voyage, the Portuguese began to establish permanent trading settlements along the coasts of eastern Africa, India, and southern Asia. This was the beginning of European colonial empires in Africa and Asia.

Quick Quiz

1. On the trip back to Africa from India, why did da Gama burn one of his ships?

2. Why do you think the Hottentots were happy with the items the Portuguese brought to trade? Why do you think the Muslim traders were insulted?

3. Reread the Look to the Source excerpt and put it into your own words. How does this passage show the dangers explorers faced? Why do you think the sailors "cried to God for mercy"?

Just for Fun!

Find the North Star

To find their way, Vasco da Gama and other explorers used the most modern navigational instruments available at the time. When explorers sailed north of the equator, they also relied on the North Star as a guide. Other names for the North Star are Polaris or polestar because it marks the location of the North Pole.

Directions:

To find the North Star, go outside on a clear night and face north. First, look for the Big Dipper, which is a group of stars that looks like a cup with a long handle. The Big Dipper is part of a larger group of stars (called a constellation) named Ursa Major. Next, find the two bright stars that are farthest from the handle of the Big Dipper. Connect the two stars and follow the line to the North Star. The North Star is at the tip of another group of stars called the Little Dipper.

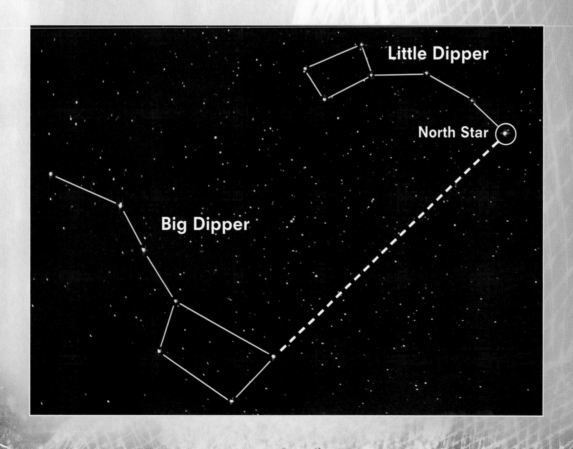

Ferdinand Magellan

asco da Gama had begun his retirement by the early 1500s, following a successful voyage to find an eastern sea route to India. Meanwhile, a young nobleman had joined the Portuguese navy and was beginning to study maps and sea charts with excitement. This young man was Ferdinand Magellan. He began dreaming of finding a new trade route to Asia by sailing west. Inspired by Henry the Navigator and Christopher Columbus, Magellan became the first man to lead an expedition that sailed around the world.

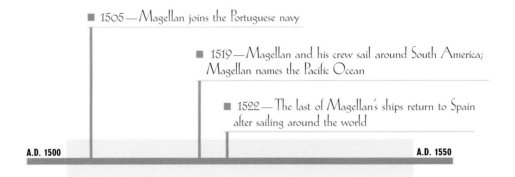

1505—Magellan joins the Portuguese navy

1519—Magellan and his crew sail around South America; Magellan names the Pacific Ocean

1522—The last of Magellan's ships return to Spain after sailing around the world

A.D. 1500   A.D. 1550

A Roman Catholic bishop once described Ferdinand Magellan as "a man of courage, [brave] in both his thoughts and in undertaking great things."

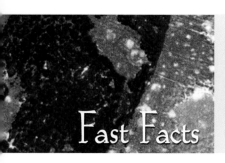

NAME: Ferdinand Magellan
BORN: 1480 in Oporto, Portugal
DIED: 1521 in Mactan, Philippines
SAILED FOR: Spain
EXPLORED: A western sea route to Asia around South America

Dreaming of a Western Route

Ferdinand Magellan was born in 1480 in Oporto, Portugal to a noble family. Magellan was the third child in his family. When he was about 12, his parents sent him to Lisbon to work as a **page** in the court of the queen of Portugal. This was an honor and also offered the boy many privileges. Most importantly, all royal pages received an excellent education. Magellan studied geography, navigation, and astronomy.

In 1505, Magellan joined the Portuguese navy and spent several years sailing the Indian Ocean. He spent many hours studying sea charts and maps. Over time, Magellan decided that he would find a sea route from Portugal to the Spice Islands in Asia by sailing west. This would be an important discovery. Vasco da Gama already had found a sea route to Asia by sailing east around the southern tip of Africa. But Magellan's dream was to sail around the world by heading west. He wanted to succeed where Columbus had failed.

page: a boy acting as a servant to someone, especially a noble person

Seeking Support

Magellan went to ask the king of Portugal for money to buy ships and supplies. However, since Portugal already controlled the southern trade route around Africa to the Spice Islands, the king refused Magellan's request. Determined to find a way, Magellan then turned to the king of Spain and made the same request. Spain had no direct route to the Spice Islands. The Spanish king decided to support Magellan's expedition. If Magellan were successful, Spain would become as rich as Portugal.

Troubles at Sea

In 1519, Magellan left Spain with five ships and about 250 sailors. His troubles began almost immediately. The Portuguese did not want Magellan to succeed because Spain was their **rival**. So, they hired workers to load empty water barrels on his ships and provide false information about how much food was onboard the ship. Magellan began his long voyage believing he had much more food and supplies than he actually did.

rival: a person or group that tries to equal or pass another

Magellan is known as the first person to sail around the world, but his own trip west ended in the Philippines. This map shows Magellan's route from 1519-1521. The waterway through the tip of South America, called the Strait of Magellan, is enlarged.

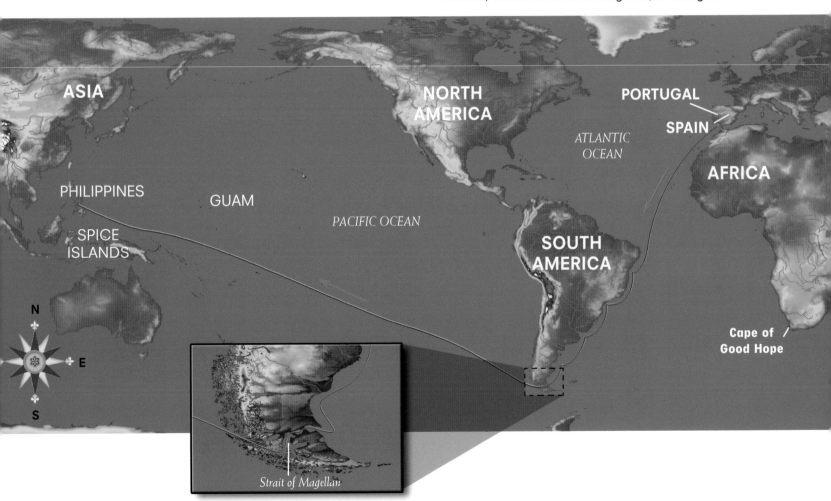

ASIA

NORTH AMERICA

PORTUGAL

SPAIN

ATLANTIC OCEAN

AFRICA

PHILIPPINES

GUAM

PACIFIC OCEAN

SPICE ISLANDS

SOUTH AMERICA

Cape of Good Hope

N
E
S

Strait of Magellan

Sailing through Uncharted Waters

Over the next several months, Magellan and his ships sailed south and west across the Atlantic Ocean. It was not an easy crossing. They ran low on food and water. Several times, Magellan's crew tried to take over his command. However, Magellan was able to maintain control. When he and his crew arrived in what is present-day Brazil, they rested and got fresh supplies before heading south along the South American coast. After weeks of trying to sail through heavy seas and cold weather, Magellan finally found a passage through the southern end of South America. Some members of his crew argued that they should return to Spain, but Magellan insisted they go on. As they sailed through the **strait** and into **uncharted** water, Magellan named the body of water *Mar Pacifico*, which means "calm sea" or "peaceful sea." The name stuck, and people have since called this body of water the Pacific Ocean.

strait: a narrow passage of water joining two larger bodies of water

uncharted: unknown or unexplored

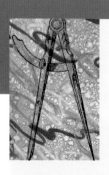

Look to the Source

Most of what we know about Magellan's voyage comes from the journal of Antonio Francesco Pigafetta. Pigafetta was an Italian passenger onboard one of Magellan's ships. Below are translated excerpts of his account of Magellan's voyage, which tell us about Magellan's character.

adversity: hardship
constant: unchanging
omit: to leave out
virtue: goodness

"Among other **virtues** which he possessed, he was more **constant** than anyone else in the greatest **adversity**. He endured hunger better than all the others, and more accurately than any man in the world did he understand sea charts and navigation."

"The Captain General [Magellan] had **omitted** ... certain particulars of the voyage to the crew, to avoid their uneasiness ... at sea."

Deadly Trip to the Spice Islands

Once they began sailing in the Pacific Ocean, Magellan thought it would be a short trip to the Spice Islands. The trip turned out to be almost four months. Many of the crew became sick and died. Finally, the ships landed on the present-day island of Guam. The crew rested and got more supplies before sailing to a group of islands known today as the Philippines.

Just for Fun!

Where in the World Am I?

The map on page 55 shows the route that Ferdinand Magellan took to Asia. Where on the map are you? Test your knowledge of geography with the activity below.

Materials:
world map with a scale (download map at www.ballard-tighe.com/readingbookactivities) • ruler • pencil • paper

Directions:
Put a mark on the world map to show the town or city where you live. This will be your reference point. On a piece of paper, write the name of this location and the answers to the following questions:

- On what continent do you live?
- Do you live on the same continent as Spain?
- What is the nearest ocean?
- What is the nearest country?
- If you traveled directly west for 500 miles, where would you be?
- If you traveled directly south for 500 miles, where would you be?

- What is your latitude? Your longitude?
- What is the nearest island?
- How far is it from where you live to the capital of the country where you live?
- How many miles are between where you live and the Strait of Magellan?
- Are you closer to the North Pole or South Pole?

Magellan discovered the sea passage around South America on November 1, the day on which many Christians celebrate the Feast of All Saints. In honor of this holiday, Magellan called the passage the Strait of All Saints. Many years later, mapmakers renamed this passage the Strait of Magellan. This modern illustration shows Magellan leading his crew through the strait and into the Pacific Ocean.

A Single Ship Returns Home

Instead of continuing toward the Spice Islands, Magellan insisted on exploring the Philippines. The king of Spain had given him orders to try to persuade the people he encountered to **convert** to Christianity. On the first island, he was successful, so he went to the next island. Unfortunately for Magellan, a battle was raging on this island between two rival groups. One of the groups was ready to convert, but the other was not. Magellan decided to use force to make this second group convert. He was killed in the battle.

convert: to adopt a new religion

ingenious: clever; showing inventive skill or imagination

After Magellan's death in 1521, his expedition experienced even greater problems. The remaining men and ships decided to go in different directions. Some sailed home, retracing the route they had come from Spain. When this did not work, they were forced to sail back to the Spice Islands. Most of these men never made it home. Others sailed toward the Cape of Good Hope. Finally, in 1522, one remaining caravel from the original five ships returned to Spain. Only 18 men had survived the journey. The Spanish forgot about Magellan and made a national hero of the captain who had brought home the last ship. It was only years later that the world became aware of Ferdinand Magellan and gave him credit for being the first to sail around the world.

Quick Quiz

1. Why did Portugal refuse to support Magellan's voyage?

2. What qualities do you admire in Ferdinand Magellan?

3. Reread the Look to the Source excerpts and put them into your own words. Do you agree with Magellan's decision not to tell his crew his entire plan for the expedition? What can you learn about Magellan from these excerpts?

Magellan was killed in a battle with a group of people he was trying to convert to Christianity. Upon Magellan's death, an Italian passenger onboard one of Magellan's ships wrote that he "was the bravest and most **ingenious** man in the world."

Jacques Cartier

nlike Portugal and Spain, at first France was not very interested in expeditions to the Americas. It wasn't until 1524 that France sent the Italian-born explorer, Giovanni da Verrazano, on a voyage to the northeastern coast of North America. It was another decade before France sent its most famous explorer across the Atlantic. In 1534, Jacques Cartier set off on an expedition to find the Northwest Passage—a sea route that connects the Atlantic Ocean and Pacific Ocean through Canada and north of Alaska.

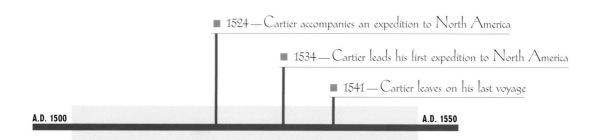

■ 1524—Cartier accompanies an expedition to North America

■ 1534—Cartier leads his first expedition to North America

■ 1541—Cartier leaves on his last voyage

A.D. 1500   A.D. 1550

Although Jacques Cartier did not discover the Northwest Passage he set out to find, he became France's best known explorer.

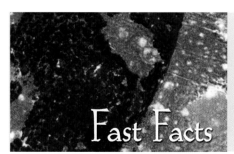

NAME: Jacques Cartier
BORN: 1491 in St. Malo, France
DIED: 1557 in St. Malo, France
SAILED FOR: France
EXPLORED: Northeastern coast of North America

A Sailor from a Sailor's Town

In the 1500s, most people who lived in the northwest coast region of France made their living as sailors, fishermen, and navigators. Jacques Cartier (kahr-tee-AY) was born in 1491 in a town in this region called St. Malo. Not much information is available about his childhood. His father was a fisherman and young Cartier accompanied him on several fishing trips off the coast of present-day Newfoundland, Canada. By 1524, Cartier had gained enough experience to accompany Giovanni da Verrazano on his voyage to the northeastern coast of North America.

Claiming Land for France

In 1533, Cartier wrote a letter to an important official in France proposing a new voyage. Cartier wanted to continue the exploration begun by Verrazano. The king of France, Francis I, agreed to Cartier's plan because he wanted to claim land for France. On a bright afternoon in April 1534, Cartier set sail with two ships and 61 sailors. His goal was to find gold as well as a direct route to Asia. After 20 days of sailing, he reached the coast of Newfoundland. Cartier and his men sailed through the Strait of Belle Isle, which separates Newfoundland from the mainland of Canada. For the next few weeks, Cartier sailed around the large bay called Chaleur Bay. He went onto land and set up a large cross and from it hung the French king's flag. By doing this, Cartier had claimed the coastal land and islands for France.

Cartier Meets the Huron

Cartier made one of his first contacts with the people who lived in the area—members of the Huron tribe—during this trip. Although the Huron did not speak French, they understood that Cartier was claiming the land. They made their objections loud and clear! In response, Cartier communicated to the Huron chief, Donnacona, that the wooden cross was only meant to mark the spot for help in navigation. Later, Cartier insisted that Donnacona's two sons return to France with him. Cartier wanted the two boys to tell the king about the land.

During his three voyages to North America, Cartier commanded a total of 10 ships. One of those ships was called *La Grande Hermine*. This illustration, created around 1923, shows an idea of how that ship might have looked.

Back to the New World

After returning to France, Cartier reported to King Francis what he had seen on his journey. The two Huron boys told stories of a river so long that no one had ever seen the end. Cartier believed that this was the Northwest Passage to Asia that he was searching for. King Francis agreed to provide support for another trip.

In 1535, Cartier began his second voyage with three ships and 100 sailors. The trip across the Atlantic Ocean was difficult because of the many spring storms. On August 10, 1535, Cartier sailed into the large **gulf** he had navigated the previous year. He named the gulf after St. Lawrence, whose life many Christians celebrate on August 10. Later, the great river that Cartier first sighted was given the same name. As Cartier continued his voyage, the chief's sons guided him up the river to their home village of Stadacona, which is the site of the present-day city of Quebec. Upon their arrival, the boys told their father that France had indeed claimed the Huron land as their own.

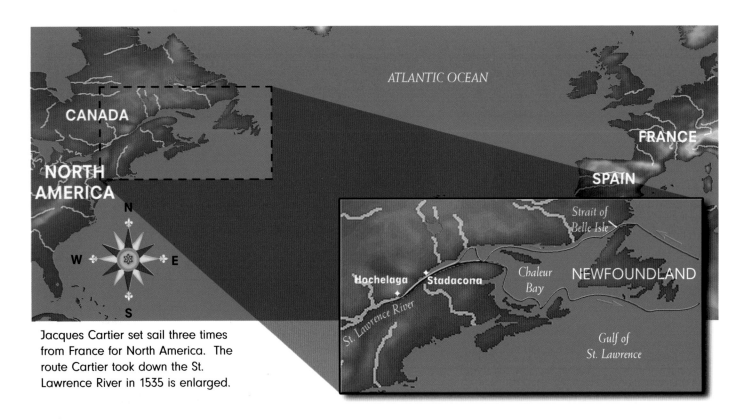

Jacques Cartier set sail three times from France for North America. The route Cartier took down the St. Lawrence River in 1535 is enlarged.

Just for Fun!

Be a Real Sailor: Learn to Tie Knots

On his second voyage to North America, Cartier encountered storms and difficult seas. During those times, it was especially important to maintain control of the ship. Like those on Cartier's expeditions, sailors throughout history have relied on knots to help manage their ships. Below are instructions for tying your own sailor's knots. You will need several long pieces of rope or string.

SQUARE KNOT: Used in folding up sails or making sails smaller. <u>Directions</u>: **1.** Hold the rope at each end. Bring ends together and pass the left end over and under the right end. **2.** Pull knot tight. Repeat Step 1, making a second loop. Pass the right end over and under the left end. Pull knot tight.

1.

2.

FIGURE EIGHT: Keeps rope from coming undone. <u>Directions</u>: **1.** Fold the rope in half, holding the middle with one hand and an end with the other. Bring the end (see A) under the standing part (see B) and then over it. **2.** Bring the end through the loop and pull the knot tight.

1.

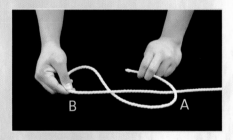

2.

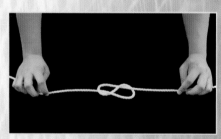

BOWLINE KNOT: Used when a reliable knot is needed; it does not untie easily. <u>Directions</u>: **1.** Hold the rope at both ends. Cross the ends so that they make a small loop (see A) in the center of the rope. Take the left end (see B) under and through the loop. **2.** Take that end and pass it over and under the other end (see C) then over and through the first loop. Pull knot tight.

1.

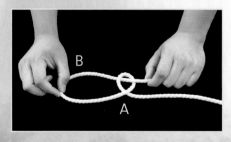

2.

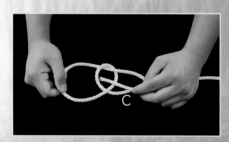

The Exploration Continues

Cartier continued his exploration of the great river beyond the village of Stadacona to a place called Hochelaga, where he believed he would find great wealth. At one point during the trip, Cartier climbed a hill and named it *Mont Réal*, which means "Royal Mount." This is how the Canadian city of Montreal got its name.

The expedition went back down the river for the winter. Even though they had built a fort, Cartier and his men were unprepared for the harsh winter. In addition to the cold, many men suffered from scurvy. The Huron showed the French how to cure scurvy with the bark of the white cedar tree. Many sailors survived the winter because of this. When the ice finally melted and his boats were able to move in the river, Cartier kidnapped Donnacona and nine other Huron and returned to France. He continued to believe treasure could be found in Canada, and he insisted the Huron tell King Francis about it.

During his exploration of the St. Lawrence River, Cartier went to a village called Hochelaga, where he thought he would find great riches. This illustration, created around 1850, shows what one of Cartier's first meetings with the Indians of Hochelaga might have looked like.

Look to the Source

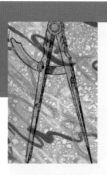

In 1589, a man named Richard Hakluyt wrote a book about Cartier's explorations. Below you can read an excerpt, which describes what happened during Cartier's third voyage in 1541. The text is translated using modern English spelling.

contrary: opposite in direction

torment: tossing and turning

victualled: having plenty of food

"Five ships set sail together well furnished and **victualled** for two years ... And we sailed so long with **contrary** winds and continual **torments**, which fell out by reason of our late departure, that we were on the sea with our said five ships full three months before we could arrive at the Port and Haven of Canada, without ever having in all that time 30 hours of good wind to serve us to keep our right course ... our five ships through those storms lost company one of another, all save two that kept together."

A New Plan

When Cartier returned to France he found the country at war with Spain. The war took all of the king's time and most of the country's money. Voyages of exploration were not as important. After several years, King Francis was willing to listen to Cartier's new plan to colonize North America. France needed money and Cartier insisted there was gold to be found in Canada. In 1541, he was ready to go on his last voyage. He was supposed to lead the expedition, but at the last moment a new leader was selected, a nobleman named Jean-Francois Roberval. Cartier did not like Roberval. When Roberval's ships were not ready on time, Cartier received permission to leave with his own five ships and 1,000 crewmen.

Cartier's Final Voyage

The expedition sailed for about three months before arriving in Canada. When Cartier arrived at Stadacona, he told the Huron that Donnacona died in France. He insisted that the other Huron had no desire to return to their country.

After spending another hard winter in Canada, Cartier left for France. As he was leaving Newfoundland, his ships encountered Roberval's group, which was just arriving. Roberval ordered Cartier to continue the exploration of the St. Lawrence River with him. Cartier knew his men would not agree to endure another winter, and he certainly did not want to take orders from Roberval! In the middle of the night, Cartier set sail and returned to France. Roberval continued his voyage up the St. Lawrence River to Cartier's abandoned fort. However, as Cartier expected, the winter was a disaster for Roberval and his men. Many of his men died. In the spring, the remainder of Roberval's expedition returned to France, without establishing a colony and without finding treasure.

Cartier never returned to Canada. He died in 1557 in St. Malo, where he lived the rest of his life. One of the consequences of Cartier's voyages was the destruction of trust between the Native Americans and the Europeans who wanted to explore their land. Jacques Cartier never found the Northwest Passage he was looking for, and he never found a treasure. But he did give France a claim to land in North America.

Quick Quiz

1. What did Cartier name the large gulf he explored? Why?

2. How did Cartier's explorations affect the relationship between Native Americans and the Europeans who wanted to explore and colonize their land?

3. Reread the Look to the Source excerpt and put it into your own words. What does this excerpt tell you about the sea voyages and the obstacles explorers faced?

More Activities

After you have read one or more of the chapters in this book, take part in one of these activities and make history come alive! You can do these on your own or with friends and family members.

PORTRAITS – Choose one of the explorers you read about in this book. Draw an outline of the person's profile.   Inside the profile, write biographical information about the person, including when he lived and why he is remembered.

ALIKE OR DIFFERENT – Choose one of the explorers you read about in this book.   Then think about how that person's life and the time in which that person lived is alike or different from your life today.   Write this information on a Venn diagram. Analyze how the two eras are alike and different, as well as how your life is alike and different from the person you chose.

A LETTER TO A FRIEND – The people who lived in the past were real people.   They enjoyed advantages, but also encountered hardships and obstacles.   Choose one of the explorers you read about in this book.   Then write a letter to a friend that starts, "I met an amazing explorer today. Let me tell you about …" In your letter, be sure to tell what you admire about the explorer, how the explorer's actions reflected his character, advantages the person enjoyed, and obstacles the person overcame.

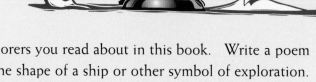

POETIC LICENSE – Choose one of the explorers you read about in this book.   Write a poem about the person on a piece of paper that is cut in the shape of a ship or other symbol of exploration. Follow the pattern below:

Line 1: The person's name
Line 2: Two adjectives to describe the person
Line 3: Three verbs to describe the person
Line 4: A sentence about the person
Line 5: The person's name

Test Your Knowledge!

1. Which of these explorers sailed for Spain?
   a. Christopher Columbus and Jacques Cartier
   b. Vasco da Gama and Amerigo Vespucci
   c. Jacques Cartier and Vasco da Gama
   d. Ferdinand Magellan and Christopher Columbus

2. On which continent is the Cape of Good Hope?
   a. South America
   b. Europe
   c. Africa
   d. Asia

3. Prince Henry the Navigator wanted to gain control of the trade in what city?
   a. Ceuta
   b. Cape Bojador
   c. Calicut
   d. Sagres

4. What group of people did Jacques Cartier meet?
   a. Bantu
   b. Arawaks
   c. Huron
   d. Hottentots

WHO AM I? (1 POINT EACH)

5. I was the first European explorer to land in the New World, but I didn't know it! I established a fort called La Navidad on the island of Hispaniola.

   Who am I? _____

6. People say that I was the first explorer to sail around the world. I sailed into the Pacific Ocean, but I never made it back to Spain.

   Who am I? _____

MAKE A MATCH (1 POINT EACH)

7. fleet	a. to adopt a new religion
8. ancestor	b. a small inexpensive ornament
9. sibling	c. something that spoils or rots easily
10. trinket	d. a group of ships
11. endure	e. unknown or unexplored
12. perishable	f. a story handed down from earlier times
13. legend	g. a family member who lived long ago
14. convert	h. to carry on despite hardships; to put up with
15. uncharted	i. brother or sister

Go to **www.ballard-tighe.com/ readingbookactivities** for more activities and ways to test your knowledge!

WHAT'S YOUR SCORE?

14-15 points – TOP SCORE!   10-11 points – Fair
12-13 points – Good   Fewer than 9 points? Read the book again!

Answers:
1-d, 2-c, 3-a, 4-c; 5-Christopher Columbus, 6-Ferdinand Magellan, 7-d, 8-g, 9-i, 10-b, 11-h, 12-c, 13-f, 14-a, 15-e

Glossary

adversity: (ad-VUR-suh-tee) *n.* Hardship.

ancestor: (AN-ses-tur) *n.* A family member who lived a long time ago.

Arab: (AYR-uhb) *n.* A person of the Arabian Peninsula.

bypass: (BIY-pas) *v.* To go around instead of going through; to avoid an obstacle.

clemency: (KLEM-uhn-see) *n.* Mercy.

colony: (KAHL-uh-nee) *n.* A group of people who settle in a land far away.

constant: (KAHN-stunt) *adj.* Unchanging.

contrary: (KAHN-trayr-ee) *adj.* Opposite in direction.

convert: (kuhn-VURT) *v.* To adopt a new religion.

custom: (KUHS-tum) *n.* The traditional way people do things.

endure: (en-DYOOR) *v.* To carry on despite hardships; to put up with.

expedition: (eks-puh-DISH-un) *n.* A trip made by a group of people for a specific purpose.

fast: (fast) *adj.* Tied or held to something securely.

fleet: (fleet) *n.* A group of ships.

Florentine: (FLAWR-uhn-teen) *n.* Someone who lives in Florence, Italy.

Fra: (fraw) *n.* Brother; a title given to an Italian friar or monk; abbreviation of the Italian word *frate*.

grief: (greef) *n.* Great sadness.

gulf: (gulf) *n.* A large area of sea or ocean partly enclosed by land.

horizontal: (hohr-uh-ZAWNT-ul) *adj.* Relating to the horizon, the line where the earth and sky seem to meet.

Iberian Peninsula (iy-BEER-ee-un puh-NIN-suh-luh) *n.* The region of southwestern Europe that is surrounded on three sides by water; present-day Spain and Portugal.

ingenious: (in-JEEN-yus) *adj.* Clever; showing inventive skill or imagination.

javelin: (JAV-lin) *n.* A spear.

knight: (niyt) *n.* During the Middle Ages in Europe, a soldier on horseback, usually of noble birth, who fought for a ruler and who was given land and privileges in return.

lament: (luh-MENT) *v.* To express sadness.

lance: (lans) *n.* A weapon with a long wooden pole and a sharp metal point.

landmark: (LAND-mahrk) *n.* A fixed marker; a large and identifying feature of a landscape.

legend: (LEJ-und) *n.* A story handed down from earlier times.

lurch: (lurch) *v.* To roll or sway suddenly, as a ship during a storm.

milestone: (MIYL-stohn) *n.* An important event or turning point in a person's history or career.

mouth: (mowth) *n.* The place where a river meets a sea or ocean.

Muslim: (MUHZ-lim) *n.* A person who follows the religion of Islam.

PARTS OF SPEECH KEY

n. — **noun; a noun is a word that names a person, place, thing, or quality**
Examples: Florentine, grief, javelin, reef

adj. — **adjective; an adjective is a word that describes, limits, qualifies, or specifies a person, place, thing, quality, or act**
Examples: constant, horizontal, perishable, uncharted

v. — **verb; a verb is a word that expresses action, occurrence, or existence**
Examples: convert, endure, lament, rely, trending

namesake: (NAYM-sayk) *n.* A person or thing named after another.

New World: (noo wurld) *n.* The Western Hemisphere; North and South America and adjacent islands.

omit: (oh-MIT) *v.* To leave out.

page: (payj) *n.* A boy acting as a servant to someone, especially a noble person.

parallel: (PAYR-uh-lel) *adj.* Always the exact distance apart; parallel lines never cross one another.

patron: (PAY-trun) *n.* A person who supports, protects, or champions something.

perishable: (PER-ish-uh-bul) *adj.* Something that spoils or rots easily.

physical geography: (FIZ-i-kul jee-AHG-ruh-fee) *n.* The study of the earth's structures and processes, including land forms, climate, and wind and ocean currents.

piteously: (PIT-ee-uhs-lee) *adv.* Sadly.

port: (pohrt) *n.* A place by the sea or ocean where boats load and unload.

rage: (rayj) *v.* To happen with great intensity.

reef: (reef) *n.* A ridge of rocks, sand, or coral that rise to or near the surface of a body of water.

rely: (ri-LIY) *v.* To depend upon or trust; to use.

representative: (rep-ri-ZEN-tuh-tiv) *n.* A person acting on behalf of the interests of another person.

rival: (RIY-vul) *n.* A person or group that tries to equal or pass another.

sibling: (SIB-ling) *n.* Brother or sister.

strait: (strayt) *n.* A narrow passage of water joining two larger bodies of water.

sultan: (SUHL-tun) *n.* The ruler of a Muslim kingdom, especially the Ottoman Empire, which began in Asia Minor in the 1300s and continued until 1922.

torment: (TOHR-ment) *n.* Tossing and turning.

trending: (TREN-ding) *v.* Turning in one direction.

trinket: (TRING-kit) *n.* A small inexpensive ornament, such as a small piece of jewelry.

uncharted: (uhn-CHAHR-tid) *adj.* Unknown or unexplored.

uninhabited: (un-in-HAB-uh-tid) *adj.* Not having any people living there.

victualled: (VIT-uld) *adj.* Having plenty of food.

virtue: (VUR-choo) *n.* Goodness.

VOWEL PRONUNCIATION KEY

SYMBOL	KEY WORDS
a	ant, man
ay	cake, May
ah	clock, arm
aw	salt, ball
ayr	hair, bear
e	neck, bed
ee	ear, key
i	chick, skin
iy	five, tiger
oh	coat, soda
oi	boy, coin
ohr	board, door
oo	blue, boot
ow	cow, owl
u	foot, wolf, bird, and the schwa sound used in final syllables followed by 'l', 'r', 's', 'm', 't', or 'n'
uh	bug, uncle, and other schwa sounds

The vowel pronunciation key is derived from the following three sources: *American Heritage Dictionary of the English Language*, 1981; *Oxford American Dictionary: Heald Colleges Edition*, 1982; *Webster's New World College Dictionary, Third Edition*, 1990.

Index

Skills Index/Credits

SKILLS INDEX

PICTURE CREDITS

TEXT CREDITS

4 *The Diario of Christopher Columbus' First Voyage to America*, 1492-1493, translated by Oliver Dunn and James E. Kelley, Jr., 1989. 13 Hale, John R., *Age of Exploration*, Time-Life Books, 1966.
22 Russell, Peter, *Prince Henry 'the Navigator': A Life*, Yale University Press, 2000. 33 *The Diario of Christopher Columbus' First Voyage to America*, 1492-1493, translated by Oliver Dunn and James E. Kelley, Jr., 1989.
34 *The Life of the Admiral Christopher Columbus by His Son Ferdinand*, translated by Benjamin Keen, Rutgers University Press, 1959. 38(t) Zweig, Stefan, *Amerigo: A Comedy of Errors in History*, Viking Press, 1942.
38(b) *Letter of Amerigo Vespucci to Pier Soderini*, translated, published at Florence in 1505-6, by "M. K." for Quaritch's edition, London, 1885. From the Internet Modern History Sourcebook, www.fordham.edu/halsall/mod/modsbook.html. 39, 40(t) Zweig, Stefan. *Amerigo: A Comedy of Errors in History*, Viking Press, 1942. 40(b) *The Letters of Amerigo Vespucci*, translated and edited by Clements Markham, Burt Franklin Publisher, 1894. 49 Correa, Gasper, *Lendas da India*, translated by Henry E. J. Stanley, the Hakluyt Society, 1869 (under the titles *The Three Voyages of Vasco da Gama*). 53, 56, 61 Parr, Charles McKew, *Ferdinand Magellan, Circumnavigato*, Thomas Y. Crowell Company, 1964. 70 *Early English and French Voyages*, chiefly from Hakluyt, 1534-1608, edited by Henry S. Burrage, Charles Scribner's Sons, 1906. Online facsimile from www.americanjourneys.org/aj-028.

Find Out More!

FIND MORE RESOURCES
on our web site
www.ballard-tighe.com/
readingbookactivities

GENERAL:

Dash, Joan. *The Longitude Prize.* New York: Farrar Straus and Giroux/Frances Foster Books, 2000. How to measure longitude remained a mystery until John Harrison, an 18th century English clockmaker, found a solution. For very advanced readers. Nonfiction.

Macaulay, David. *Ship.* Boston: Houghton Mifflin, 1993. This book includes everything you ever wanted to know about caravels, the space shuttles of the 15th century. Nonfiction.

PRINCE HENRY THE NAVIGATOR:

Hurwicz, Claude. *Henry the Navigator.* New York: PowerKids Press, 2000. This is a short, easy-to-read biography. You won't find detailed information, but it provides a good general outline of Henry's life and work. Nonfiction.

Simon, Charnan. *The World's Great Explorers: Henry the Navigator.* Chicago: Childrens Press, 1993. This is a detailed biography of Prince Henry in the context of Europe's age of exploration. Lots of maps, photographs, illustrations, and other colorful visuals. Nonfiction.

CHRISTOPHER COLUMBUS:

Conrad, Pam. *Pedro's Journal: A Voyage with Christopher Columbus August 3, 1492-February 14, 1493.* New York: Scholastic, 1992. This book of historical fiction tells the story of Columbus's voyage from the perspective of young Pedro de Salcedo, a ship's boy on the *Santa María* who keeps a journal of his experiences. Fiction.

Fritz, Jean. *Where Do You Think You're Going, Christopher Columbus?* New York: Paper Star, 1997. This easy-to-read book tells the story of Christopher Columbus who was looking for a new route to the Indies, but found a whole new world. ALA Notable Book, School Library Journal Best Book of the Year, Booklist Notable Children's Book of the Year. Nonfiction.

AMERIGO VESPUCCI:

Alper, Ann Fitzpatrick. *Forgotten Voyager: The Story of Amerigo Vespucci.* Minneapolis, MN: Carolrhoda Books, 1991. This book discusses how forged letters played a role in the naming of the continents of the New World. Nonfiction.

Donaldson-Forbes, Jeff. *Amerigo Vespucci.* New York: PowerKids, 2003. This book describes Vespucci's explorations in the New World. Easy to read. Fiction.

VASCO DA GAMA:

Gallagher, Jim. *Vasco Da Gama and the Portuguese Explorers.* New York: Chelsea House, 2000. This is a well-written biography of the great Portuguese explorer with helpful information about the time in which he lived. Nonfiction.

Stefoff, Rebecca. *Vasco De Gama and the Portuguese Explorers.* New York: Chelsea House, 1993. This book focuses on the achievements of the Portuguese explorers, including such notables as Prince Henry the Navigator and Vasco da Gama. Nonfiction.

FERDINAND MAGELLAN:

Gallagher, Jim. *Ferdinand Magellan and the First Voyage Around the World.* New York: Chelsea House, 2000. This book tells the story of Ferdinand Magellan in a concise way with many helpful visuals. Nonfiction.

Metzler, Milton. *Ferdinand Magellan: First to Sail Around the World.* Tarrytown, NY: Benchmark Books, 2001. This is an interesting biography of the man who is credited with being the first to sail around the globe. Nonfiction.

JACQUES CARTIER:

Blashfield, Jean F. *Cartier: Jacques Cartier in Search of the Northwest Passage.* Minneapolis, MN: Compass Point Books, 2001. This is an easy-to-read, colorful biography of Jacques Cartier. Nonfiction.

Harmon, Daniel E. *Jacques Cartier and the Exploration of Canada.* New York: Chelsea House, 2000. This is an easy-to-read biography of Jacques Cartier, the man who claimed land in North America for France. Nonfiction.

Acknowledgments

any people contributed their knowledge, talents, and enthusiasm to this book. We are indebted to a remarkable editorial staff, especially Kristin Belsher, and including Heera Kang and Patrice Gotsch. We also are indebted to Liliana Estep, the art director of the *Explore the Ages* series, and to Ronaldo Benaraw, the talented graphic designer for this book. They brought to life our ideas about pairing text and visuals and the result is more beautiful than we thought possible. We are grateful for helpful comments and suggestions on earlier drafts of this work by Dr. Diane L. Brooks, Dr. Cheryl Riggs, and David Vigilante. This book is dedicated to Biscuit, Luca, and Gemma, our own intrepid explorers.

Roberta Stathis & Gregory Blanch

Dr. Stathis is an educator, writer, and editor. Dr. Blanch is on the faculty at New Mexico State University. They are co-authors of People and Stories in World History: A Historical Anthology *(Ballard & Tighe, 2003) and the other books in the* Explore the Ages *series—*Leaders Who Changed the World, Women Who Ruled, Renaissance Artists Who Inspired the World, *and* Writers Who Inspired the World *(Ballard & Tighe, 2004).*